# Manchester Quiz Book

C000010780

## 101 Questions To Test Your Knowledge Of This Prestigious Club

Published by Glowworm Press
7 Nuffield Way
Abingdon OX14 1RL

By Chris Carpenter

## Manchester City Football Club

This book contains one hundred and one informative and entertaining trivia questions with multiple choice answers. You will be asked many interesting questions on a wide range of topics associated with **Manchester City Football Club** for you to test yourself. With 101 questions, some easy, some challenging, this book will test your knowledge and memory of the club's long and successful history.

You will be quizzed on players, legends, managers, opponents, transfer deals, trophies, records, honours, fixtures and more, guaranteeing you both plenty of fun and an educational experience. This Manchester City Quiz Book will provide the ultimate in entertainment for Man City fans of all ages, and will test your knowledge of the club.

# 2022/23 Season Edition

# FOREWORD

When I was asked to write a foreword to this book I was flattered.

I have known the author Chris Carpenter for a number of years and his knowledge of facts and figures is phenomenal.

His love for football and his skill in writing quiz books make him the ideal man to pay homage to my great love Manchester City Football Club.

This book came about as a result of a challenge on a golf course.

I do hope you enjoy the book.


Terry Hamilton

Let's kick off with some relatively easy questions.

1. When was Manchester City founded?
   A. 1872
   B. 1876
   C. 1880

2. What is Manchester City's nickname?
   A. The Blue Devils
   B. The Citizens
   C. The Toffees

3. What is the club's record attendance?
   A. 82,695
   B. 83,956
   C. 84,569

4. Who or what is the club mascot?
   A. Abdul the Sheikh
   B. Captain Canary
   C. Moonchester and Moonbeam

5. Who has made the most appearances for the club in total?
   A. Joe Corrigan
   B. Mike Doyle
   C. Alan Oakes

6. Who has made the most League appearances for the club?
   A. Eric Brook

B. Joe Corrigan

C. Alan Oakes

7. Who is the club's record goal scorer?
    A. Sergio Aguero
    B. Eric Brook
    C. Tommy Johnson

8. Who is the fastest ever goal scorer for the club in the Premier League?
    A. Sergio Aguero
    B. Jesus Navas
    C. Carlos Tevez

9. Which of the following song do the players run out to?
    A. Blue Bayou
    B. Blue Monday
    C. Blue Moon

10. Which of these is a well known pub near the ground?
    A. The Barbers Shop
    B. The Bottle Shop
    C. The Corner Shop

OK, so here are the answers to the first ten questions. If you get eight or more right, you are doing very well so far, but you should know the questions will get harder.

A1. Manchester City was founded in 1880.

A2. Manchester City's official nickname is the Citizens, although they are also known as the Sky Blues, and City.

A3. Manchester City's record home attendance is an incredible 84,569 for an FA Cup match against Stoke City at Maine Road on 3rd March, 1934. This is a record for the highest home attendance in English football.

A4. The club mascots are Moonchester and Moonbeam. The alien couple are regularly seen in the family section of the stadium and are happy to have their photographs taken.

A5. Alan Oakes made the most appearances for the club. He played in 676 first-team matches from 1959 to 1976.

A6. Alan Oakes, with 561 League appearances holds the record for the most League appearances for the club.

A7. Sergio Aguero is Manchester City's record goal scorer with 254 goals in all competitions, as at 1st September 2020.

A8. Jesus Navas scored just after 13 seconds against Spurs on the 24th November 2013 to become the club's fastest ever goal scorer in The Premier League era.

A9. The players run out to 'Blue Moon'. It was written by Rodgers and Hart way back in 1934. It has been recorded by many artists including Frank Sinatra, Ella Fitzgerald and Elvis Presley, although arguably the most famous version is by The Marcels.

A10. The Corner Shop is a well-known pub near the ground. Be prepared to queue for a pint though.

OK, back to the questions.

11. Where does Manchester City play their home games?
    A. City of Manchester Stadium
    B. Emirates Stadium
    C. Sky Blue Lane

12. What is the stadium's capacity for domestic football games?
    A. 55,017
    B. 55,170
    C. 55,701

13. When was the last match played at Maine Road?
    A. May 2002
    B. May 2003
    C. May 2004

14. What is the name of the road the new ground is on?
    A. Ashton New Road
    B. City Road
    C. Millennium Way

15. When did the club move to the City of Manchester Stadium?
    A. 2003
    B. 2004
    C. 2005

16. What is the size of the pitch?
    A. 112x72 yards
    B. 114x74 yards
    C. 116x77 yards

17. Who were the first band to play a concert at the stadium?
    A. Oasis
    B. Red Hot Chili Peppers
    C. Take That

18. Where is Manchester City's training ground?
    A. Banana Ridge
    B. Carrington
    C. Etihad Complex

19. What is the highest number of goals that Manchester City has scored in a league season?
    A. 104
    B. 106
    C. 108

20. What is the largest number of clean sheets kept in one season by a Manchester City goalkeeper?
    A. 27
    B. 28
    C. 29

Here are the answers to the last set of questions.

A11. Manchester City play their home games at the City of Manchester Stadium, which is also known as Eastlands, and also the Etihad Stadium since July 2011 due to a large naming rights sponsorship deal. At the risk of being controversial, it is the only football stadium in Manchester, as Old Trafford is in Salford.

A12. The current stadium capacity is 55,017 for football matches in domestic matches, and under UEFA regulations it is capped at 53,000 for European matches.

A13. Maine Road, the so called Wembley of the North, was home for Manchester City from 1923 until its last match on 11th May 2003.

A14. The Etihad Stadium is on Ashton New Road.

A15. The club moved to the City of Manchester Stadium in 2003, with its first competitive game taking place on the 14th August 2003.

A16. The size of the pitch is 116 yards long by 77 yards wide. By way of comparison, the pitch at Wembley is 115 yards by 75 yards.

A17. The first concert at the stadium was by the Red Hot Chili Peppers on 18th June 2004. The stadium is one of the UK's largest concert venues, and artists that have performed there include Bon Jovi, Coldplay, Oasis, Ed Sheeran, Bruce Springsteen and U2.

A18. Manchester City's moved their training facilities to the Etihad Complex - a purpose built £200million facility in the east of the city in December 2014. It is without doubt the best football club training facility in the UK.

A19. Manchester City has scored 108 goals in two seasons - 1926/27 in the Second Division and 2001/02 in the Championship. In the Premier League era, the club scored 106 goals in just 38 games in the 2017/18 season.

A20. In the 2010/11 season Joe Hart managed to record an incredible 29 clean sheets for the club.

Here is the next set of questions.

21. What is the club's record win in any competition?
    A. 11-2
    B. 12-0
    C. 13-1

22. Where was Bernardo Silva born?
    A. Italy
    B. Spain
    C. Portugal

23. Who started the 2022/23 season as manager?
    A. Pep Guardiola
    B. Brian Kidd
    C. Manuel Pellegrini

24. What is the club's record win in the league?
    A. 9-1
    B. 10-2
    C. 11-3

25. Who is the current director of football at the club?
    A. Mohamed Al Mazrouei
    B. Txiki Begiristain
    C. Ferran Soriano

26. In the late 1908s what inflatable objects were often seen at City home games?
    A. Apples
    B. Bananas
    C. Pears

27. What is the club's official twitter account?
    A. @ManCity
    B. @ManchesterCity
    C. @MCFC

28. What was ex-manager Joe Mercer's nickname?
    A. Generous Joe
    B. Gentleman Joe
    C. Genuine Joe

29. Where was Erling Haaland born?
    A. England
    B. Norway
    C. Sweden

30. Who has scored the most hat tricks for Manchester City in the Premier League era?
    A. Sergio Aguero
    B. Robinho
    C. Carlos Tevez

Here is the latest set of answers

A21. The club's record win in any competition is 12-0 when the club beat Liverpool Stanley 12-0. Yes, that really was their name. The match took place on 4th October 1890, so it is the 1890/91 season.

A22. Bernardo Silva was born in Lisbon in Portugal.

A23. Pep Guardiola started the 2022/23 season as manager. He was appointed in February 2016, taking the role of manager at the start of the 2016/17 season.

A24. The club's record win in the league is 11-3, a victory over Lincoln City on 23rd March 1895.

A25. Aitor "Txiki" Begiristain is the current director of football at the club.

A26. In the late 1980s City fans started a craze of bringing inflatable bananas to matches! They were even sold in the club shop at the time.

A27. @ManCity is the club's official twitter account. It tweets multiple times daily and it has over thirteen million followers.

A28. Joe Mercer's nickname was Gentleman Joe.

A29. Erling Haaland was born in Leeds! At the age of three, he moved to his parents' hometown ion Norway.

A30. Argentinian striker Sergio Aguero has scored a record twelve Premier League hat tricks for the club.

Now we move onto some questions about the club's trophies.

31. How many times have Manchester City won the League?
    A. 6
    B. 7
    C. 8

32. How many times have Manchester City won the FA Cup?
    A. 5
    B. 6
    C. 7

33. How many times have Manchester City won the League Cup?
    A. 4
    B. 6
    C. 8

34. When did the club win their first League title?
    A. 1926/27
    B. 1936/37
    C. 1946/47

35. When did the club win their first FA Cup?
    A. 1904
    B. 1924
    C. 1934

36. When did the club win their first League Cup?
    A. 1960
    B. 1970
    C. 1980

37. Who was the last captain to lift the League trophy?
    A. Fernandinho
    B. Vincent Kompany
    C. Yaya Toure

38. Who was the last captain to lift the FA Cup?
    A. Tony Book
    B. Vincent Kompany
    C. Carlos Tevez

39. Who was the last captain to lift the League Cup?
    A. Kevin De Bruyne
    B. Fernandinho
    C. David Silva

40. When did the club win their only major European trophy?
    A. 1960
    B. 1970
    C. 1980

Here is the next set of answers.

A31. Manchester City has won the League 8 times. (1936/37, 1967/68, 2011/12, 2013/14, 2017/18, 2018/19, 2020/21 and 2021/22)

A32. Manchester City has won the FA Cup 6 times. (1904, 1934, 1956, 1969, 2011 and 2019)

A33. Manchester City has won the League Cup 8 times. (1969/70, 1975/76, 2013/14, 2015/16, 2017/18, 2018/19, 2019/20 and 2020/21)

A34. Manchester City won their first League title in the 1936/37 season.

A35. Manchester City won their first FA Cup in 1904. City defeated Bolton Wanderers 1-0 in the FA Cup Final held at Crystal Palace on 23rd April 1904

A36. Manchester City won their first League Cup by beating West Bromwich Albion 2-1 at Wembley on 7th March 1970.

A37. Fernandinho, in his last game for the club. was the last captain to lift the League trophy; at the end of the 2021/22 season.

A38. Vincent Kompany was the last captain to lift the FA Cup, at Wembley on 18th May 2019 after City beat Watford 6-0.

A39. Fernandinho was the last captain to lift the EFL League Cup, at Wembley on 25th April 2021 after City beat Tottenham Hotspur 1-0.

A40. On 29th April 1970, Manchester City defeated Polish side Gornik Zabrze 2-1 in the European Cup Winners Cup Final in Vienna. This is the club's only major European trophy win. So far.

I hope you're having fun, and getting most of the answers right. Here is the next set of questions.

41. What is the record transfer fee paid?
    A. £60 million
    B. £80 million
    C. £100 million

42. Who was the record transfer fee paid for?
    A. Jack Grealish
    B. Riyad Mahrez
    C. Rodrigo

43. What is the record transfer fee received?
    A. £34.8 million
    B. £44.8 million
    C. £54.8 million

44. Who was the record transfer fee received for?
    A. Leroy Sane
    B. Raheem Sterling
    C. Ferran Torres

45. Who has won the most international caps whilst a Manchester City player?
    A. Gareth Barry
    B. Colin Bell
    C. David Silva

46. Who has won the most international caps
    for England whilst a Manchester City
    player?
    A. Colin Bell
    B. Joe Hart
    C. Francis Lee

47. What is the club's official website
    address?
    A. mancity.co.uk
    B. mancity.com
    C. mcfc.com

48. Who is the youngest player ever to
    represent the club?
    A. Tommy Booth
    B. Glyn Pardoe
    C. Paul Power

49. Who is the oldest player ever to represent
    the club?
    A. Joe Corrigan
    B. Mike Doyle
    C. Billy Meredith

50. Who was the captain who lifted the
    European Cup Winners Cup in 1970?
    A. Tony Book
    B. Mike Doyle
    C. Alan Oakes

Here is the latest set of answers.

A41. Manchester City paid £100 million for an English midfielder in August 2021.

A42. The record fee of £100 million was paid to Aston Villa for Jack Grealish. It eclipsed the previous record fee of £62.8 million paid to Atletico Madrid for Rodrigo in July 2019.

A43. The record transfer fee received by Manchester City is £54.8 million.

A44. The fee was received from Bayern Munich for German winger Leroy Sane in July 2020.

A45. David Silva is the record holder here, having won over 80 of his 125 caps for Spain whilst at Manchester City. As he is a current player, this number will continue to increase.

A46. Colin Bell won a total of 48 caps for England, but he takes second place to Joe Hart who won more than 60 caps for the national side.

A47. mancity.com is the club's official website address.

A48. Glyn Pardoe is the youngest player ever to represent the club. He made his first team appearance at the age of 15 years, 314 days against Birmingham City on 11th April 1962.

A49. Billy Meredith is the oldest player ever to represent the club. He appeared for the club at the ripe old age of 49 years 245 days against Newcastle United in the FA Cup on 29th March 1924.

A50. On 29th April 1970, Manchester City beat Gornik Zabrze 2-1 in the 1970 European Cup Winners Cup Final in Vienna. Tony Book was the captain who lifted the trophy that glorious night.

I hope you're learning some new facts about the club,

51. When was the MCFC Official Supporters club formed?
    A. 1939
    B. 1949
    C. 1959

52. Who is the club's longest serving manager of all time?
    A. Peter Hodge
    B. Roberto Mancini
    C. Wilf Wild

53. Who is the club's longest serving post war manager?
    A. Tony Book
    B. Les McDowall
    C. Joe Mercer

54. What is the name of the Manchester City match day programme?
    A. Manchester City official matchday programme
    B. Manchester City diaries
    C. City

55. Who started the 2022/23 season as club captain?
    A. Kevin de Bruyne
    B. Ilkay Gundogan

C. Kyle Walker

56. Which of these was a Manchester City fanzine?
    A. Blue Skies
    B. King of the Kippax
    C. Manchester City Diaries

57. What animal is associated with the club, and used to be on the club crest?
    A. Bald Eagle
    B. Golden Eagle
    C. Harpy Eagle

58. What is the club's motto?
    A. Consectatio Excellentiae
    B. Nil Satis Nisi Optimum
    C. Superbia in Proelio

59. Who is considered as Manchester City's main rivals?
    A. Bolton Wanderers
    B. Manchester United
    C. Liverpool

60. What could be regarded as the club's most well known chant?
    A. Blue Is The Colour
    B. Blue Moon
    C. Blue Murder

Here are the answers to the last set of questions.

A51. The MCFC Official Supporters club was founded in 1949.

A52. Wilf Wild is the club's longest serving manager of all time, serving as manager from 1932 to 1946. His tenure covered the whole of the Second World War when no competitive games were played, and he was in charge for a total of 352 matches.

A53. Les McDowall is the club's longest serving post war manager. He served from 1950 to 1963 and was in charge for a total of 592 matches.

A54. The name of the Manchester City match day programme is imaginatively entitled 'City'.

A55. Ilkay Gundogan started the 2022/23 season as club captain.

A56. King of the Kippax was probably the best known Manchester City fanzine.

A57. Manchester City's old badge was based on the arms of the city of Manchester, and the crest consisted of a shield in front of a golden eagle.

A58. The Latin motto of Manchester City is 'Superbia in Proelio'. It means 'Pride in Battle' in English.

A59. Manchester United is of course City's main rival.

A60. 'Blue Moon' can be regarded as the club's most well known chant. All together now "You saw me standing alone..."

Let's give you some easy questions.

61. What is the traditional colour of the home shirt?
    A. Midnight blue
    B. Royal blue
    C. Sky blue

62. What is the traditional colour of the away shirt?
    A. Maroon
    B. Pink
    C. Red and black stripes

63. Who is the current club sponsor?
    A. Emirates
    B. Etihad Airways
    C. Gulf Air

64. Who was the first club shirt sponsor?
    A. Phillips
    B. Saab
    C. Thomas Cook

65. Which of these companies once sponsored the club?
    A. Brother
    B. Mother
    C. Uncle

66. Who is currently the club chairman?
    A. Abdul el Khabib

B. Ahmed Mubarak
C. Khaldoon Al Mubarak

67. Who was the club's first foreign signing?
    A. Walter Bowman
    B. Herbert Burgess
    C. David Phillips

68. Who or what was the Kippax?
    A. An Asian speciality, like a shish
       kebab
    B. A stand at Maine Road
    C. A localised rain storm

69. Who was the club's first match in the
    Football League against?
    A. Accrington
    B. Bootle
    C. Grimsby Town

70. How many times has Pep Guardiola won
    the Premier League Manager of the Season
    award?
    A. 2
    B. 3
    C. 4

Here are the answers to the last block of questions.

A61. The traditional colour of the home shirt is of course sky blue.

A62. The colour of the away shirt is nowadays maroon, but traditionally it was red and black stripes if you're old school. Award yourself a point for either answer.

A63. Etihad Airways is the current sponsor of Manchester City.

A64. Saab was the first shirt sponsor of Manchester City. They sponsored the club from 1982 to 1984.

A65. Technology company Brother sponsored the club from 1991 to 1999.

A66. Khaldoon Al Mubarak is the current club chairman.

A67. Canadian Walter Bowman was the club's first foreign signing. He signed for City in 1893 and he was the first non-British player to play in the Football League.

A68. The Kippax was the best known, and most vocal of the stands at the old Maine Road stadium, named after Kippax Street which ran alongside the ground. Unofficially the East Stand in the new stadium has been named Kippax.

A69. The club's first match in the Football League was against Bootle. The match was played on 3rd September 1892, and City won 7-0.

A70. Guardiola has won the Premier League Manager of the Season award three times.

Here is the next batch of ten carefully chosen questions.

71. Who has scored the most penalties in a season for the club?
    A. Tony Book
    B. Dennis Law
    C. Francis Lee

72. Who won the PFA Young Player of the Year award in 1974/75?
    A. Peter Barnes
    B. Francis Lee
    C. Mike Summerbee

73. When did the club become the first team to be automatically promoted to the First Division from the Second Division?
    A. 1886
    B. 1889
    C. 1892

74. Who holds the record for the most clean-sheets for the club?
    A. Joe Corrigan
    B. Shay Given
    C. Joe Hart

75. Who played in the 1956 FA Cup Final with a broken neck?
    A. Eric Brook
    B. Joe Corrigan

C. Bert Trautmann

76. Which former City goalkeeper was killed
    in the Munich Air disaster in 1958?
    A. Eric Kite
    B. Frank Swift
    C. Albert Thrush

77. What was the transfer fee paid for
    Robinho in 2008?
    A. £30.5 million
    B. £32.5 million
    C. £34.5 million

78. What mode of transport appears on the
    club crest?
    A. An Aeroplane
    B. A Ship
    C. A Train

79. Who was the first Manchester City player
    to win the Footballer of the Year award?
    A. Alan Oakes
    B. Don Revie
    C. Bert Trautmann

80. Which country does Riyad Mahrez play
    for?
    A. Albania
    B. Algeria
    C. Argentina

Here is the latest set of answers.

A71. Francis Lee holds the record for most penalties scored in a season for the club. He scored 13 times from the penalty spot in the 1971/72 season.

A72. Peter Barnes won the PFA Young Player of the Year award for his performances in the 1974/75 season.

A73. The club became the first team to be automatically promoted to the First Division from the Second Division way back in 1889.

A74. Joe Hart holds the record for the most clean-sheets for the club, with 18 in the 2012/13 season.

A75. Bert Trautmann played in the 1956 FA Cup Final with a broken neck.

A76. Frank Swift was tragically killed in the 1958 Munich Air disaster.

A77. £32.5 million was paid to Real Madrid for Robinho on 1st September 2008. It was a signing that demonstrated the club had changed for ever.

A78. The current badge, which was unveiled on 26th December 2015 is circular in design. The badge features a ship on its upper half representing the Manchester Ship Canal and on the lower half there is the red rose of Lancashire and three diagonal stripes which symbolise the city's three rivers - the Irwell, the Irk and the Medlock  I told you this book would be informative, and you'd learn something new!

A79. Don Revie was the first Manchester City player to win the Footballer of the Year award. He won this prestigious award at the end of the 1954/55 season.

A80. Winger Mahrez plays for Algeria.

Here are the next set of questions, let's hope you get most of them right.

81. Who was the first non-European manager of the club?
    A. Sven-Goran Eriksson
    B. Roberto Mancini
    C. Manuel Pellegrini

82. What transfer fee was received for Mario Balotelli?
    A. £15 million
    B. £17 million
    C. £19 million

83. Who managed Manchester City for just 33 days?
    A. Steve Coppell
    B. Asa Hartford
    C. Tom Maley

84. How many times has Richard Dunne won the Supporters' Player of the Year Award?
    A. 2
    B. 3
    C. 4

85. Who scored the winning goal in the 2011 FA Cup Final?
    A. Mario Balotelli
    B. Aleksandar Kolorov
    C. Yaya Toure

86. How much did the club sell Raheem Sterling for?
    A. £37.5 million
    B. £47.5million
    C. £57.5 million

87. Who has scored the highest number of goals in a season for the club?
    A. Peter Doherty
    B. Tommy Johnson
    C. Alan Oakes

88. Who among the following was a part of "The Holy Trinity" of the club along with Colin Bell and Francis Lee?
    A. Mike Doyle
    B. Mike Summerbee
    C. Neil Young

89. What shirt number does John Stones wear?
    A. 4
    B. 5
    C. 6

90. When did Manchester City both score and concede 100 goals in the same season?
    A. 1953/54
    B. 1955/56
    C. 1957/58

Here are the answers to the last set of questions.

A81. In July 2007, Sven-Goran Eriksson became the first non-British Manchester City manager. However, Chilean Manuel Pellegrini was the first non-European manager of the club taking charge in June 2013.

A82. £19 million was received for Mario Balotelli from A.C. Milan in January 2013.

A83. Steve Coppell was appointed City manager in October 1996, and managed just six games in his 33 days in charge.

A84. Richard Dunne won the Supporters' Player of the Year Award four times, continuously from 2005 to 2008.

A85. On 14 May 2011 Manchester City defeated Stoke City 1-0 to win their fifth FA Cup. The only goal of the game was scored by Yaya Toure.

A86. In July 2022 Manchester City sold Raheem Sterling to Chelsea for £47.5 million.

A87. Tommy Johnson scored 38 goals in the 1928/29 season.

A88. Mike Summerbee, Colin Bell and Francis Lee were together known as "The Holy Trinity".

A89. John Stones now wears the number 5 shirt.

A90. In the 1957/58 season Manchester City scored 104 goals and conceded 100 goals. They finished fifth in the League.

Here is the final set of questions. Enjoy!

91. Which famous Mancunian musician
    supports Manchester City?
    A.  Gary Barlow
    B.  Ian Brown
    C.  Liam Gallagher

92. When was Manchester City relegated to
    the Third Division for the first time?
    A.  1990
    B.  1994
    C.  1998

93. Who scored a goal for City in a 1-0 win
    against Manchester United to confirm the
    relegation of their rivals in the 1973/74
    season?
    A.  Denis Law
    B.  Francis Lee
    C.  Uwe Rosler

94. What shirt number did David Silva wear?
    A.  19
    B.  21
    C.  27

95. What was Manchester City called when
    the club was formed?
    A.  Ardwick
    B.  St. Mark's
    C.  West Gorton

96. Who is nicknamed "The Engineer"?
    A. Mark Hughes
    B. Brian Kidd
    C. Manuel Pellegrini

97. When did Manchester City become the first club to be relegated with a positive goal difference?
    A. 1933/34
    B. 1935/36
    C. 1937/38

98. Who was known as "The Wizard of Longsight"?
    A. Sam Coppell
    B. Roberto Mancini
    C. Sam Ormerod

99. When was Manchester City purchased by the Abu Dhabi United Group, making it one of the wealthiest clubs in the world?
    A. 2004
    B. 2006
    C. 2008

100. Who was nicknamed "Nijinsky" and also "The King of the Kippax"?
    A. Colin Bell
    B. Shaun Goater
    C. Denis Tueart

Here is the final question, and it's a good one.

101. Who scored the winning goal in injury
time in the last game of the 2011/12
season to enable Manchester City to win
the Premier League for the first time?
   A.  Sergio Aguero
   B.  Edin Dzeko
   C.  Yaya Toure

Here is the final set of answers.

A91. The Gallagher brothers, Liam and Noel are avid supporters of Manchester City.

A92. Manchester City was relegated to the Third Division for the first time in May 1998. Dark days indeed.

A93. Denis Law scored the only goal for City in a 1-0 win against Manchester United to confirm the relegation of their rivals at the end of the 1973/74 season.

A94. David Silva wore shirt number 21.

A95. Manchester City FC was called St Mark's when the club was formed. The club was founded in 1880 as St. Mark's (West Gorton), it became Ardwick Association Football Club in 1887 and Manchester City in 1894.

A96. Manuel Pellegrini is nicknamed "The Engineer".

A97. Manchester City became the first club to be relegated with a positive goal difference at the end of the 1937/38 season.

A98. Sam Ormerod was known as "The Wizard of Longsight". Sam managed the club from 1895 to 1902 and it was he who got the club promoted to the top league for the first time.

A99. Manchester City was purchased by the Abu Dhabi United Group on 1st September 2008. Things have certainly changed since the take-over.

A100. Nicknamed Nijinsky after the famous racehorse (due to his renowned stamina), Colin Bell was also "The King of the Kippax" and played a total of 394 games, scoring 117 goals for the club. In 2004 the club polled supporters to name a new stand for the new stadium. Colin Bell won with an overwhelming majority and the West Stand was thus renamed The Colin Bell Stand in honour of City's greatest ever player.

A101. Who could ever forget Sergio Aguero scoring the winning goal in one of the most memorable moments in football history ever, scoring deep into injury time in the last match of the season against QPR on 13th May 2012 to help Manchester City win the Premier League for the first time.

That's it. That's a great question to finish with. I hope you enjoyed this book, and I hope you got most of the answers right.

I also hope you learnt some new facts about the club, and if you spotted anything wrong, or have a general comment, please visit the glowwormpress.com website and send us a message.

Thanks for reading, and if you did enjoy the book, would you please leave a positive review on Amazon.

Printed in Great Britain
by Amazon

22080331R00030